SHE IS

ART

She Is Art

This is your reminder
You are everything you've ever needed.

a female embodiment

She Is Art

She Is Art

A POETRY COLLECTION
By Madison Farraway

She Is Art

Disclaimer:
This book contains explicit mature content and language.

Formatting, poems
cover and Illustration made by Madison

ISBN: 978-1-7388770-7-2

Madison Farraway
Canada, Ontario

Maddocumentspoetry.contact@gmail.com
www.maddocuments.com

She Is Art

CONTENTS

She Is Art

CHAPTER ONE

girlhood is morally an act of immorality

reborn

i marked that garage door with a pencil to mark a
place where i stay
i expected the door and ceiling to intertwin
i expected all my questions to be answered
but i've yet to outlive girlhood
girlhood it is the pit
i am flesh and we are reborn continuously

suddenly it was cold
snow covered the grounds
i said goodbye
i kissed you one last time
took one last look at a place i considered home
with a tear rolling down my cheek i got into that car
and thought about all the more i could have said
i didn't know that would be the last time i'd walk
through those doors
or that it would be the last time i'd trace my finger
down those walls ever again
but most of us don't know
when something will be our last time
most of us don't know when it will be our last
goodbye

   -   *somewhere i considered home*

i blew out the candles

my birthday was last week
i blew out my candles
i devoured that cake like it would be my last
i turned the age i always dreamed of being as a child
it's nothing how i thought
its empty
it's cold
it's dark here

mind over matter

as the warmth of the sun beats down upon my skin
i hear the birds chirping and it fills this void within
i realized at this moment nothing else matters
because nothing ever really matters outside of this
very moment
that is what i find peace in
that is what keeps me grounded

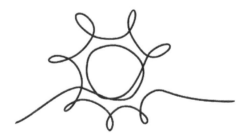

i feel so uneasy
as if my mood could be changed in a second
as if everything i have ever wished and dreamed for
could be taken away from me
at the cost of one thought

-   *and it was*

a innocent act

are you mad at me is the questions she got
"you're everything i want,"
"i'm going to marry you,"
"you're everything i've ever needed"

and although these sound sweet to her
although these probably sound sweet to you too
it is nothing but pure evil
because if you look closely enough
it is only ever "i'
it's never what do you want
never what do you need?
never, are you okay?

he said he cared
but his care was only ever care for himself
a benefit to himself
he says all of this in the name of love
as he slides his hand down her pants

romanticizing the torment, girlhood

you said i looked cute when i cry
with my red spots covering my face and
bejeweled tears
romanizing me even in my saddest moments

you said it was cute when i'd scream in frustration
and anguish being captured through the lens of a
mans camera
as my bones begin to show
my eyes darken and my hair begins to thin

cute he says
romanticizing the torment
girlhood

cheers to getting older

we were young girls
as much as we wanted to be anything more than that
anything more than little girls we weren't

we sat at our park bench drinking blue slushies with
five hour energy drinks soaked within
pretending to be drunk
pretending to be grown
cheers to getting older we said

everyone is home

home
everyone is home

often home is four walls and a roof but as a child
home was your mom cooking dinner
while dads in the garage
your siblings are outside
and everyone is home

until you outlive childhood
you no longer hope everyone is home
you begin to forget the feeling of everyone being
home and the smell of your favorite dinner in the
midst of that warm summer

mean girls

and from neighbors
to friends
to enemies
you spit words of poison on me
you talk down on me
expecting me to fall

you take my clothes and call them yours
perhaps it's jealousy
at least that is what my counselor said

"*best friends*"

she always put out little jokes when other girls
complimented her i mean they were friends
best friends
but as she began to talk about her presents she was
so eager to get for christmas
a blank flat toned emotionless expression
grew on her face

and they talked about the boys they liked
they spent most lunches together
she always ate too fast when she was hungry
she'd have this look written upon her face
a look that could be straight out of a mean girls
movie

there was something about her
there was something about her she wanted gone
but they were best friends

the denim skirt

from grade school
to middle school
just about everyone had their people
everyone but her

she sat alone for lunch most days
she didn't have a fully prepped lunch like the other
kids
she didn't have the newest shoes or clothes but she
wanted to

so she worked till she saved up for the newest in
style denim skirt like all the other girls
maybe then they would like her

she was so excited
but as she entered that classroom
only to see all the faces she feared most
they'd laugh
"what is it about me that is so unlovable?" she says

today a little girl looked at me
only this look seemed too familiar
her eyes lit up as she walked by
and i smiled because i knew soon enough
she would be everything she looked up to
she soon enough she would be all grown up
i understood her because i was her
not long ago

girlhood

girlhood
she can wear pretty dresses
she can put her hair into braids
girlhood
she gazes at the mirror
over analyzing every inch of her body
obsessing over every imperfection
the intensely painful beauty of seeing it all demolish

the pretty dresses make men stare at her legs
scanning her body head to toe
girlhood
everything you do
say and wear is a fetish
a prize for men to bathe in
the knowledge no matter how innocent your
intentions are perceived
in man's world there is no escape
but in the sisterhood of appreciation only us woman
share this universal hurt
girlhood

i will chase the feeling of you forever
i must miss being in flames

you say you love me

you think you love me
you know the shape of my body
the touch of my skin but

what's my favorite thing to do
or do you only know what i like to do with you
what's my favorite song
favorite color
what was my childhood nickname

what keeps me up at night when you're asleep
what are my weaknesses
what about my strengths
what do i value
who do i value
tell me about my childhood…

i don't think you love me
i don't think you can love me
how do you love someone you don't know

i had convinced myself that i deserved it
that i deserved all the things happening
beneath the surface
deeper than i could ever grasp

you will never be that child again
you will never get to experience those feelings you
once did at least not like before
it is gone

we were all drowning together
we didn't know how to swim
but we had each other

- *if only you knew how lucky i was to have you
  beside me*

She Is Art

She Is Art

CHAPTER TWO

adolescent love

your perfection

it's fucking sick isn't it
i've been 90 pounds
i've been 150 pounds
i've had a waist of 19 inches
no matter how light i get
it is dark here
the pursuit of your perfection
consumes me
consuming every thought
every memory

anyone can fall in love
but maybe we don't truly fall in love
maybe we only fall in love with a dream
a fantasy
a image that our minds so creatively create

i lived off the idea
that just maybe one day
you'd feel the pain
you had so deeply imbedded within me
that maybe one day you taste the poison you
poisoned me with

it is okay, he loved her

it starts young
small pokes
little jokes
mean jokes
it was okay, he only likes you

he grabs her chest
he lifts her skirt
he takes pictures sending them off
rubbing her thighs up and down
as he talks soft to her
it was okay, he loved her

he yelled
he screamed
he hit her
it was okay, he said he's sorry

maybe tomorrow

maybe tomorrow she will be better
her clothes
they sit scattered upon her room
they've been there for weeks
she's tired
she's sad
she tired after she sleeps for 10 hours
she is exhausted beyond all measures
she looks in the reflection of the mess she has
become and is yet to outgrow
"i'm fat, im ugly" she says
she is downing
she is drained
but maybe tomorrow she will do better

-    teenage depression

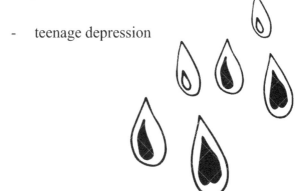

isolation

my world
my reality
i shelter my peace
where not a soul can harm it

isolation isn't good they say
i disagree
i've never been happier
never been more present then when i am alone
i've grown to be comfortable alone
maybe too comfortable

- *peace*

i blocked all my friends

she blocked her friends
she deleted their numbers
because they tell her to be less
when she is more

she blocked her friends because they only reach out
when it is convenient to them

she blocked all her friends because
she hears their whispers as she walks up upon them

she blocked all her friends because
on a sidewalk she stands behind them

she blocked all her friends
because they made her feel less, when she wanted to
be more.

love yourself

learn to be alone
learn to run alone
learn to workout alone
learn to succeed alone
learn to be comfortable alone

you know i love you

she was the "i hate you" kind of girl
he was the "you know you love me" kind of boy
they would joke and tease each other

but this isn't a love story

because then after he said "i hate myself"
she laid there upon his grave and whispered
"you know i love you"

-    *and i loved you*

i love you most

when i say i love you more
i don't mean i love you more than you love me
i mean i love you more
then the bad days ahead of us
i love you more than any fight
we will ever have
i love you more than the distance between us
i love you more than any obstacle that
could ever try and come
between us
i love you the most

you are what i have been searching for

home
a place where you are supposed to feel loved
a place you are supposed to feel comfortable
a place i've longed for
home
you are my home
you are what i have been searching for

you are the love i'd live for

i didn't want to be the kind of love you'd die for
i wanted to be the kind of love you'd live for

girlhood was going to the park
spilling ice cream on that pink shirt you'd wear one
to many days in a row
pepto bismol for the anxiety induced stomach
girlhood is hugging every little girl you meet
girlhood is smelling wood chips at the park
and eating cheese and crackers in the pool
then a forced nap after

girlhood is crying all night in the dark
girlhood is drawing on your arm
girlhood is telling your mom when you got your first
period
girlhood is wildly full of softness and sadness
but truly what is girlhood without
grief of that boy you loved

- *sweet n' sour*

he must love me

i went out with my friends
he got mad said i should be home at 10
he pulled my shorts down and gave me his hoodie
told me to cover up
how sweet he's so protective

yesterday he got really mad
it was the first day of school
i asked a boy to help me in class
it was cute how jealous he got

he took my phone
he threatened that boy
he yelled at me
he punched the walls
he must really love me

i stopped hanging out with my friends
i only hangout with him
but i guess this is what love is
he must really love me

"you can keep the door open, but you don't have to stand there holding it,"

you can keep the door open for him but don't stand there waiting for him

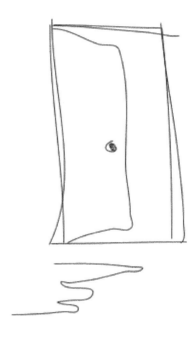

you know that deep feeling of sadness
that takes over your body
when you once think back to what you once had
the deep longing for love that is no longer there

-    *the distance between us*

is a loving relationship that is slowly falling apart.

i soothe myself to sleep
i trace the freckles on my face
i hold myself when i cry
i drink from bottles when i'm thirsty
and eat pills when i'm hungry
i set enough alarms to make
the whole house go crazy
alone and cold on my floors
i count the hours
and watch the days dwindling away
i lock my thoughts in a compartment
that no one can reach
i rewind the clocks
to when i was something more to you

sometimes

sometimes
she still finds herself subconsciously
absent-mindedly thinking about you
sometimes it still hurts
and she hates that she still thinks about you
they say forgive but don't forget
but she would wipe out every memory of you
if she had the choice
she would forget you entirely
she would turn her back
and never think of you for a second
her head and her heart are not aligned
because in her head she almost hates you
but her heart wants to look past all the bad
and continue to love the person you once were
a person that is no longer

the thing about us is
it is different
but different in the best way possible

do not let the inconsistent love from others
make you addicted to when they do decide to show
their temporary love

- *temporary highs and consistent lows*

you're mad
you're angry
you're sad
but you need to understand
that hating someone
hurts you more than anyone

-   *you will heal*

i like your imperfections

i like your hair
the way you part it
i like the color of your eyes
i like the slope of your nose
i like that your body is so perfectly imperfect
i like everything you over analyze about yourself
i like every part of you that you call ugly
i like that your sensitive
i like your insecurities

you are perfect and i know you don't see it right now
but i promise in 15 years time
maybe 20 you will look back and see it too.

to build a home

a house and a home
are very similar but very different
they appear to be the same to one looking in
but a home is a place that holds comfort within
a place to hide when the world seems a little too loud
but to me home was you

hard to love

your words leak like a faucet
telling me you love me
but your actions show different
i believe i never knew you all along
or maybe i was just blinded by your love
i'd rather be alone
then alone with you
you've made it seem as if loving me
was so hard to do

you cannot continue to see past the red flags
to see the good in those people
it's not fair to you
it's not even fair to them

he had touched me again
after months without
his touch
his smile
his arms around me
it felt like home
it felt like the person he once was come back
i wanted to hate it
i knew it wasn't a good thing
i wanted to feel nothing
yet it felt like i could breathe again
after what felt like a lifetime without air

they would hurt each other
most of the time out of anger
but they loved each other

so they stayed in a toxic cycle
and found themselves addicted
continuing to breaking one another
calling it love

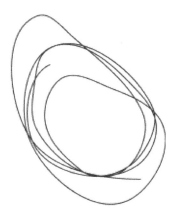

it is not that it was ever a good relationship
it was broken sometimes
and seemed whole at others
they'd fight and yell
argue and hold grudges for days
it was never a good relationship
it was never healthy or strong
however above all this it was the only bond she
seemed to know
they would crumble and fall
then rise as if nothing had even happened

with the right person
you will not have to beg to be heard
you will not have to beg to be loved
you will not have to beg to feel seen

an attachment

i would drain every ounce of blood from my
veins if it granted you eternal mercy
i would break every bone in my body if it
gave you everything you most desire
i would give up my mind and all of my
beautiful thoughts to receive your affection
i would do all of this in
the name of love that was the problem

i could have had anything
in this world
but all i wanted was you

   -   *and you left*

she once called him home

and eventually you weren't a person
eventually you were a chore
a task one would dread to complete
a burden that is something to stand in my way '
something to weigh me down
you never treated me like a person
i don't think i am much of anything
at all when i'm with you
all i ever wanted was you
all i ever wanted was to be something to you

i loved you until
those words felt meaningless

loving you was much like walking
along the train tracks
knowing a train was ahead

i wanted to rip out your chapter in my book
only to realize
i would be ripping out a part of my story

a lie that made me feel clean

i have you implanted in my blood
we were broken
you poisoned my tongue
while i said words i didn't mean
"i love you"
"i hate you"

i am not that naive

the most heartwarming tear rolling part of all of this
is no one will ever be you i will find other people
i'm not naive there were ones before you and will be
ones after
other men to hold me, kiss me and love me, ones to
sit and talk for hours about life with
i know, life goes on
but what am i supposed to say
when the next guy i stand beside
asks me why i left and my tears begin to roll
he doesn't know about the scars or the bruises
he doesn't hold me, like you did but
maybe he'll take me for a fancy dinner dates
open my car door
maybe my family will adore him
i know i will find someone
someone to love me in ways you couldn't
someone a smile alone can satisfy
i'm not that naïve
but i also know i will spend the rest of my time
drainingly translating myself
fully knowing that you spoke my language

he said a part of him would always love her
that's not what she wanted him to say
because if he hated her
maybe she would hate him too

She Is Art

CHAPTER THREE

i hate you,
i love you

in love with a ghost

when you told me heartbreak feels like
mourning a loved one or like someone died
you were wrong
it is so much more
so much worse
death is final
but this
this isn't final

your still here
they still talk about you
i still hear you
and i still feel you
there is nothing final about being in love with you
mourning a lost
grieving a loved ones passing is love that has
nowhere to go
but loving you is like loving a ghost
a ghost that's not really dead
and knowing that makes it so much more
so much worse

i hated being a woman for most of my life
it came with more rules
and responsibilities than i had expected
i thought that being a woman meant this world was
always going to be hard to navigate
as if i would never find out the unspoken rules of
womanhood that isn't taught–but expected to know
i thought this world was never aligned to be a place
where i could thrive
where women are viewed as a possession
as something to own
something to fear if i'm ever alone

but i am grateful for the intuition and the connections
i love everything that men will never understand
about being a woman
i love the power woman hold
i love being able to love a woman in a way a man
could never
womanhood is indecisive
it is moody
it is full of laughs, cries and all the inbetween
womanhood, i wouldn't change anything about it

she wants you to let her be feminine

she wants you to let her be feminine
she wants to feel allowed to be feminine
she wants you to make her feel safe
she wants you to save the last cookie for her
she wants you to plan dates
she wants you to provide clarity
she wants to know in a room full of people you will
always look for her
she wants you to let her be led by everything she
carries naturally
she wants to feel safe
she wants to feel like she is allowed to be a woman

let me be the words within this book
where the ink stains our names on every page
let us be trapped within
they say nothing lasts forever

but this
this is forever
our love is forever
together or strangers it will always be

she longed to feel loved deep down
she made herself untouchable
she'd hope that one day for this storm to settle
she clenched her pillow full of bejeweled tears
imaging this is what it felt like to be loved

-   *and hoped it wasn't as cold as this*

what if i only feel alive when i'm with you
what if my world only eases when you hold me
what if when i'm with you
i feel at home but the thing about that is you can rip
it away so easily
then suddenly i don't know who i am
a world surrounded by you
a world revolved around you

you can't make homes out of people
well you can but you shouldn't because now i made
a home out of you and now that you're gone
where do i go
now that i don't feel loved by you
i feel i am nothing

full
i feel full
my heart is full
but not swollen because of sorrow or lost love
full as if i have found a new compartment within
there is so much to fill
and i am doing it easily with you

how is she supposed to love someone
so intensely
so innocently
and unconditionally after
you tainted her love

they weren't lying when they said life goes on
it does it went on
it just wasn't the same
but it does go on

i handed you the gun

they say to love someone is to hand them
a loaded gun and trust them not to pull the trigger
and i handed you the gun
you unloaded the clip
empted the magazin
using me for target practice
convincing the mess you had made of me was
perfection
writing me the villain and you the victim
in your story
i write about you as if you put the stars in the sky
you say you love me
but you only love how i love you
you left me in a blindfold i created from your toxic
love i then saw the mess you made

you touch my skin to make me feel alive
i taste your lips against mine
and my hair stands on end when i see you
your eyes light up but
full of hidden hunger and evil
i would tell you how i feel but
your eyes whisper "i know"

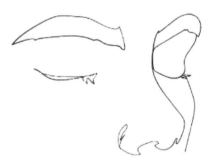

i had the match

i looked into your eyes
told you i loved you
knowing everything we once had
had been burned to a flame
with nothing but ash left
and you whispered i had the match

i'll never be anything more then body to you
as if he was uninterested of knowing about all that
lies so deeply within
"i want to be heard"
"i want to feel heard"
"i don't want you to pretend to love me just to have
the most intimate parts of me" she says

"i wanted you to love me"
"i wanted a reason to feel like it is okay to love"
but you showed her why she can't
becoming numb giving you what you want
and romanticizing the torment
romancing a man wanting her for something other
than her body
hoping that one day his lust would manifest into
something more

maybe in another universe
you loved me the way i needed you to love me
maybe in another universe you held me when i need
you to hold me
i longed to feel loved by you
because somewhere between now and then you did

you told her you loved her
deep down she knew you didn't
maybe she knew it wouldn't be anything more
maybe deep down she didn't want
it to be anything more
but that's not how she wanted you to feel
what was it that made her so unlovable

- *egotistical*

she wanted you

on the surface
she didn't want you but deep down
she wanted you
she wanted you to make her feel
like she was allowed to love
she wanted you to make her feel
like she was allowed to trust you
she wanted you to care
she wanted to feel wanted
she wanted you
she wanted all of you
she wanted you to love her

-   *she wanted to feel safe*

unlovable

i wanted you to want me
i wanted you to want something other than my body
i wanted you to want all the pieces of me
i thought were unlovable

you fear every person after him will hurt you
you can't love without being petrified
that they are going to hurt you like he did
you don't think you'll ever love anyone
well at least not like how you loved him
you're scared that everyone will use
and abuse you like he did

-   *but, i promise they won't*

you want to love but you're scared
because you're use to loving people
who only find you desirable for sex
you don't think you are someone
who anyone can truly love
you think you are unloveable
and so you're afraid
because it scary for him to come along and love all
the parts of you that you don't even love
you think you are too toxic
you think you have too much baggage
you think you're too difficult
for someone to love you
but i promise you're not

he says
i loved you
and i swear you loved me too
perhaps you only held me because
you only wanted someone to hold
with him on your mind
yet all i wanted was you
and my lips were just convenient

-   *from his perspective*

it feels like we were together yesterday
unbeknownst to you
we have had conversations
in my head everyday
since you've been gone

- *i miss you*

if you want to love me
love me kindly
love me whole
but do not love me half
do not love me with doubt or hesitation
love me whole

i have drainingly spent my whole life
trying to get people to understand my language
and you understand it effortlessly

she watched his attention drift
his eyes and mind drift off
fantasizing over other women
she was okay with it
she would fantasize about being with a man
that her smile alone
could satisfy one who only needs her

she does everything she did with you
trying to create and mold you
into another person
to feel the love she once shared with you
to feel you again

- *i still look for you amid everyone
and everything*

you will never be happy if you keep searching
for happiness within another person

-     *you will never live*
  if you are living for another person

you cannot beg them to like you
you cannot beg them to love you
you cannot force them to be in your life

if they wanted to be here with you, they would
you are worth so much more than wasting your time
on someone who doesn't see the value in you

"yet all i wanted was him"
but he isn't here anymore love

-   *he's gone*

when he left you

when he left you you turned off your emotions
the void within you grew
and you tried to fill that void
maybe it worked for a bit but
you need to understand
you do not miss him
or his love
you miss the potential

-    *let him go*

you have forgotten what it feels like to be alone

you're not lonely
you just don't have them
you spent your entire life with a man
and now that you don't have one beside you to kiss
you before bed
you feel incomplete
lost
unfulfilled
you spent your entire life with a man
and now you have forgotten
what it feels like to be alone

when she gave herself to you
when she gave you her heart
knowing you could rip it to two
knowing you could break such a fragile part of her
but that was what she was willing to give
to gain you

it's admirable
it truly is
to voluntarily hand over such a precious part of you
while saying "i'm willing for you to break me"

-   *and that's exactly what you did*

you were manipulative
but i loved you
you spoke bitter words to me
but i loved you
your eyes full of hunger and evil
but i didn't care
i loved you
you ripped me apart and i stayed
because i loved you

in order to love yourself

in order to love who you are now
you need to stop hating
the experiences that made the best of you
the worst of you and everything in between
of who you are today
who you were yesterday
and who you will be tomorrow

i hoped one day it would turn into love
we bit our tongues
hoping for it to manifest into something
i loved you and i swear you loved me too
perhaps you only loved the way i loved you
perhaps you just wanted to feel love
something you chased the entirety
of your life to feel
in the end we never spoke again
but all i ever wanted was you

a high school crush

his love story isn't typical
more than friends but less than what most may think
making do with their stolen glances
and hidden hugs
knowing they could never be anything more
knowing they shouldn't be anything more

- *more than friends but less than lovers*

if they jumped off a cliff

if they'd jump off a cliff would you follow
something we've all heard
something all our parents said
we shook our heads and sighed

but if you jumped off a cliff
i'd be falling with you
and i would hope this fall would go on
because then i would have the time to tell you
i love you on your worst days
and on your best days
but above it all

- *i've loved you most all along*

she is art

you do not need to understand poetry
to admire the beauty it holds within, but it helps
to understand the meak set of feelings
that is held under the surface.
the words stretch and contort my body,
it gorges me,
it breaks me,
it makes me whole.
a sense of healing
a sense of feelings that only these words capture.
it helps when you understand poetry but,
you don't need to understand it to read it.
a man can admire a woman's beauty
without engaging with her mind.
searching for the validation from these men that fail
to pick apart the internal differences
from one woman to the next.
the feeling of not being enough for a man that only
knows lust, a man thirsty for something
only a woman's body can hydrate.
she is art
i can hang her up in a art gallery
and not one man would think to get to know
her beyond what his eyes can see.
but it only takes one man,
to see the beauty that is held within.

i'm fine

im fine
she says
she wasn't fine

an emptiness consumes her as those words
leave her lips
she cries in hopes it will fill the void within

in hopes for him to crawl into her arms
in hopes he will be able to read all that her mind has
hidden

parts of us are still burning

you were busy with someone new
i thought i was done expecting all the good and bad
but turns out parts of us are still burning
parts of me still want to feel again
parts of me want to feel you again

his perfection

in a world you are expected to be feminine
before human
she would love to not become consumed
to what we have created as a society

everytime she says "i am not like other girls"
she contradicts herself
as her femininity was made for his amusement
as she alterers herself to intertwin with his idea
of feminine his idea of perfection

a ghost of a soul i onced loved

she always dismissed the bad days
the good days made up for it

she hated the way it changed you
how it locked you away
you'd always tell her you'd kill her
if she ever come close to it
she always forgave you
no matter how empty it made her

you withering away as time went on
becoming an emotionless being
voiding any feelings left
and decaying from the inside out
pieces of you slowly chipped away
until you were an empty shell of the person you once
were until she could no longer recognize you
fragments of you fade
till nothing remained but an echo
a hollow resemblance
now unrecognizable
a ghost of a soul she once loved

when it's right
you won't always be questioning
if it is

forced energy, isn't worth it

he will do what he wants to do
let him do him
if he doesn't want to make plans with you let him
if he doesn't want to reply to you
hours or days later let him
if he wanted to put effort into you he would
allow it
let it be
his action will show you how much he respects you
from there it's all up to you

- *do not lose yourself to gain him*

for as long as i can remember
it was me
only me

alone
i like being alone
it gives me a form of peace that people can't
but for the first time ever
i want someone else's company other than my own
that is what makes you different

stolen glances

i sutter the words of what is meant to speak
i have no perfect words to be spoken
i cannot take your pain
but i'd run a million miles to save you from it
let me help you let it go
i am not perfect
i am not who i appear to be
but please hold on to me
maybe i'm not enough
maybe if i could speak the right words
your world wouldn't be so tough
but hold on
hold on for me
put the pain away and let us be

i never knew kissing you
would make me forget the world
so easily

knowing you was always easy
but falling in love with you was hard
the possibilities that surrounded me

possible outcomes
i knew these consequences were my risk to take
so i took the risk to be with you
losing myself to love you was my risk to take

-   *and i did*

i sit here
rotting away
what am i doing
"they don't value you"
i think to myself
would you look to see the good on my worst days
would you still love me when my lips
are dry and when i don't get out of bed for days on
end when i pray for raining days only to stay inside
and sleep for 15 hours
god i want to be loved so badly
but the idea we are able to love but choose to be
toxic leaves my heart and stomach intertwined

- *i want to be loved*

i didn't care that i was getting a fraction
of what i deserved
because a fraction of you
was better than nothing at all

we never exchanged i love yous
but we knew

i believe deep down
she knew the answers
she just wasn't ready to accept it

loving it feels so good
until it doesn't
until you begin to hide away
blocking out every feeling you once had
every feeling you could have
until every memory
every thought is turned off

- *when they broke your heart*

being with you is like drowning
except you were the one holding me down and every
time i came up for air
i wasn't scared or even angry
i was overjoyed just to see your face before you
pushed me back into the water
until i didn't come up for air

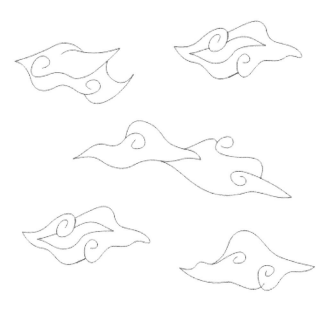

toxic is "love"

home is fire
and he felt like home she says
she looked into the flames burning from within his
eyes and managed to feel the warmth from within
he was home
because home always felt like it was in flames and
he never convinced her love is was anything
more anything other then toxic
when she meets someone new
and their eyes don't have flames
she knows she is incapable to love as something
feels that it is missing

- *addictive*

she didn't value the intimate parts
of such a intimate act
because then if she did
how would she survive in a world full of empty
people that feed off of one another's bodies without
the knowledge of their name

-   *the art of fear*

nothing was ever said anything about you
even after you were gone
you didn't deserve it
but i was so scared
to tarnish your reputation
but what i didn't realize was that i was putting her in
danger
because the longer i was silent
the longer you were able to do everything to her
that you did to me

she felt as if
he threw her so far away from herself
she often wonders if she will never return

then you lied

she began to knock her walls down for you
she began to throw herself away for you
and everything she most desired
then you lied

"letting down your walls gives them a handbook on
exactly how to hurt you"
something she's heard one too many times
but i guess she thought it would be different
this time that you could be different

-   *and you weren't*

CHAPTER FOUR

the void of womanhood

you told her to let go
only it is your rope that is tied around her wrist
your hands that grip her neck
your breath that sends shivers down her spine
and your lips that paralyze her

she would give anything to be okay
to go back to the way it once was
she felt you slowly pull away
and become more distant
you fell more and more out of love with her
less and less "i love yous"

was it your way of preparing her to live without you
why did you promise her everything
if you didn't plan on keeping those promises
yet it's still you that she wants

what could i have done to change it you asked
nothing there was nothing you could have said
there was nothing you could have done
sometimes people just fall out of love

-   *if it's meant to be they will come back*

You cannot expect the answers
if you do not explore the question

i miss feeling like you liked talking to me
i miss when i was more than just a toy
to play with whenever you pleased
it's not that i don't love you
i just can't stand the way
i shrink while you grow
i just can't stand the stinging handprints
you left embedded within my soul

it's not that i don't love you
i just can't stand the love you never gave me
it's not that i don't love you
i just can't stand the faucet of
emotions you drain by saying my name
it's not that i don't love you
i can't understand why i still do

faded

i fell in love with you because
i have never felt the love
i felt with you
the things you didn't even know you were doing
that's what made you so special
yet so different
you drifted away

knowing there was nothing
i could have done to stop it
you were gone
even if i don't like it
i have never felt the love i felt with you
even if it ended up breaking my heart

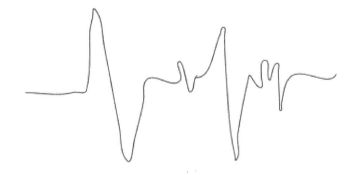

we built this home, and burned it

we built walls
they were so high
the walls we hid each other within
full of love

you lit your cigarette and flicked the ash
watching it burn
turning our walls to crumble
knowing the hours that quickly turned
to days and nights were being thrown away with the
walls we built
there was no saving us

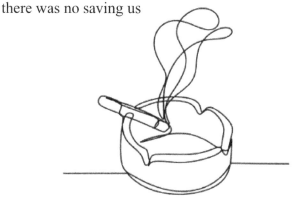

"i love you" you said

you didn't love her
you loved the idea of her
you loved the love she gave you
you loved that she was there every time you fell
and you knew she'd be there to pick you up
you loved that you could hurt her
and you knew she wouldn't leave
you loved having control of her
it made you feel powerful
but you said you loved her

"i need you to hate me"

"i love you," you said,

i dreaded it every time
"i need you to hate me"
because if you hated me then i could hate you
but the words never came out
 "i love you too" i said

you hurt me
you broke me
you made me feel like nothing
i didn't understand but i would still sit there
and act like you were the best thing that ever
happened to me
i would sit there
and still wish you all the happiness in the world
even after the hurt
even with tears in my eyes

i know you were to good to be true

you were too good to be true
you were always so good to me
i know you loved me
i know you stayed on the phone to hear me breathe
i know you placed a band-aid over wounds in me
you did not cause

i know but what else you loved me
making it seem you were doing me a favor
i know you stayed on the phone to hear me breathe
to ensure i enjoy no one else's company
i know you placed a band-aid over my wounds
wounds you did not cause only to rip it off at your
convenience i know
you were too good to be true

she didn't leave because
she stopped loving him
she left because the longer she stayed
the longer she poured her whole heart out
for him to show she loved him enough
to stay she was no longer there
she no longer loved herself

her heart was addicted to pain
because it kept beating for him
trapped in the cycle of forgiving his lies
knowing he would never change
eyes were too blind to see their "love" was just a
mirror image she created in her mind
because she was afraid of the reality
afraid of the person she knew deep down he was
she allowed him to seduce her with empty promises
and empty lies but
she is longer a novice thanks to him

he was her world everything was him
he was her everything
in the end he broke her heart
he had her wrapped around his finger
much like a string you know when you were a kid
and you would wrap your hair
around your finger or the string that
would come out of your clothes
till the tip of your finger turned purple
much like that
she was wrapped around his finger
and he still broke her
and it's still him she loves

people ask why i lock myself in my room
and cover my walls in writing
i cannot tell you why
other than i have to
it may not look like poetry
like broken things usually do
some people come in and cry blue tears
when they get close enough to read it
i have a thing
subconsciously letting my mind
run to places it shouldn't
at least that's what i discovered from the young age
of eight i've never been good at spelling but i swear
on the bones of my broken dreams
that words hurt me in my sleep
if you ask me what it feels like to
drown within them instead of trying to swim
i use my words to describe

-   *poetry*

it is not the pain
it is not the memories
or the trail they left behind that breaks her
it is what they could have been built
had they stayed

as everyone starts to fall asleep,
i go to places no one can touch me

at least not when i'm alone
walking clothed at night
i'm bathed in blood
i close my eyes and smile
and say "you all know you deserved it"

they say love makes us do crazy things
seems as if they were right

- *she whispers as she steps off the ledge*

i call to hear you
hear your voice
to feel the comfort again
even if it is just for a glimpse of a minute

why is it so hard to remain friends
why is it still your touch
i find myself searching for

i don't think she will ever love another
not like the way i loved him she says
i miss who he used to be
i miss who i thought he was
i miss the person i thought i loved
i miss his touch she says

- *in the end she never did love anyone not like
how she loved him*

i don't think i'll ever forget you
or the way you made me feel
but maybe that's our forever
the only forever we were supposed to have

- *forever*

the first love you tell your child about

she had to go through the humbling experience
of him not loving her the way she loved him
to wake up from a false reality
her mind had created
was convincingly very creative
to think they could have been anything
more than the love story they tell their kids
when they have their first heartbreak

she was always the one that would leave and move
on but then she met him and for some reason
she stayed when she should've left
i guess she just felt something different
something she never felt before
something that she felt more potential within
he used her to give him
the love and reassurance he chased his whole life for
she let her guard down
and he hurt her and let them hurt her

i realized i had started to change myself
the longer i stayed with you

-   *a story in fourteen words*

it was too late when i realized
"when he said i'm scared of hurting you
it wasn't empathy, it was a warning."

she knew he was going to hurt her
she saw it
she felt it
but once she realized
it was too late
on her lowest days
she thinks about the love they once had
or the love she thought they had
the days it was only them

she thinks about you
and she hopes what you found love in
gave you what were searching for
and she hopes you found comfort
contentment and peace
she hopes it makes you happy

- *she hopes the best for you after all*

stop breaking your own heart by trying to make a
relationship work that isn't meant to work
you can't force someone to care about you
you can't force someone to be loyal
you can't force someone to be the person
you need them to be
sometimes the person you want most is the person
you're best without
you have to understand somethings
are meant to happen
somethings are meant to come into your life
and not meant to stay
don't lose yourself by trying to heal
what's meant to stay broken
don't try to make him the one
when you know he is not
love doesn't work like that

a person who values you
would never put themselves in a situation where
they could lose you

sometimes you have to sit back
and realize you did everything in
your power for them
and all it did was hurt you
all they did was hurt you

the right attention from
the wrong person during a lonely time
can and will trick you
into thinking they're the one

i spent half my time loving you
and the other half hiding
how much i loved you

silence often holds more answers than words
it will provide more peace
when words become too overwhelming to express

most relationships don't end
because they stop loving each other
they end because one
stopped putting in the effort
that was once there
the attention
communication and security they needed

you can not force someone to communicate
and work things out
you cannot beg someone to see that
your love is worth fighting for

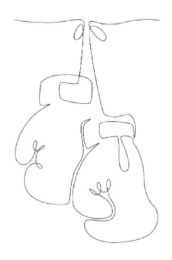

i was once told
people who struggle to let go
and hold onto things they know shouldn't
it is because that was one thing
that only made them happy

love it affects your mood
affects you from the inside and out
and that's the worst part about love
that no matter how much you try it still hurts
and it still feels like everything
you do isn't enough

i now know
you don't get to keep everyone
there are some people that are there to pull you
out of the tunnel
friends
relationships that are temporary
no matter how deep of a conversation you had with
them at 3am or how much truth you spoke
that you would never share with anyone else
if you can still draw the lines of there face
like the map of a too familiar road
there will come a time to move on
a time to let go
but no matter of letting go
you will always feel a little like home to me

you are losing me
everytime i look at you i love you a little less
and when you kiss me well i hate when you kiss me
i still wonder how your day was
but i don't dwell on the fact that i won't know
i don't get those butterflies
when i look at you anymore
i stopped wondering if you were thinking of me
i am accepting that i am drifting away from you
and maybe that is better

- *let them lose you*

love
one day you will find someone that loves you the
way you need to be loved
you will find someone
the right one
but for now take this time as a gift
learn to be there for yourself
and love yourself the way you need to be loved

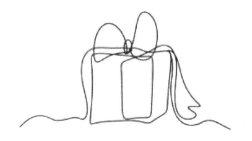

if i could forget them
if i could make more room for your love
i would
unfortunately the space that you still hold within me
is the parts i would never change
and the parts i love most

- *to the next boy*

the most real connections take place
when one is deeply connected to themselves

you do not need them
to apologize for all they did to you
it's beautiful to get it
but you know how painful
it was when you experienced it
you do not need them to
give you permission to feel it

the one who broke you cannot heal you
someone who has the power to destroy you
and uses that power
why would you trust them with rebuilding you

you deserve the more than the world
don't settle for less

they check in on you to see if you're happier without
them and you know they always said you would be
they said a lot of things
to make you love you them
to make you hate you them
you lost who you were trying to keep them
moving on doesn't mean you have forgotten
it doesn't erase what you had
but it allows room for you to be loved by someone
who deserves to love you
if you weren't meant for him then that means you
must be meant for someone else too
the good thing about letting them go
means you get another chance
for someone to love you right

- *and you deserve to be loved right*

if he cared
he would change

if he cared
he would call

if he cared
he would be with you right now

he doesn't care
but he's all you care about

- *somethings aren't fair*

love shouldn't hurt
love shouldn't bring out the worst in you
screaming to be heard
and begging for the bare minimum
but only to find out
you don't mean as much to them
as they do to you
put the walls up
push them away
why fight for something that was gone
a long time ago or never there to begin with

-   *let them go*

sometimes the only closure you need
is knowing you did what you could
to the best of your ability
even if it wasn't enough

Stay single until you find someone who can match your loyalty. Stay single until you find someone who can reciprocate your effort. Stay single until you find someone who can give back the same amount of attention you put out. Stay single until you find someone who can make the same amount of time you share. Stay single until you find someone who provides the same level of honesty you exploit. Stay single until you find someone who meets all of your expectations as clearly as you've set them. If you're single right now, it's not because you're not enough. It's not because nobody feels the same way about you. It's not because you're bad at relationships. It's because no one is ready for you just yet, it's because they are the ones who don't deserve someone like you. It's because you aren't settling for just anybody who tells you that they care. Yes, it does get lonely seeing other couples being happy together doesn't make it easier. Even seeing other couples argue may make you miss being in a relationship because the thought of having someone who cares deeply enough to fight with you and fight for you is what hits you. Loving yourself, empowering yourself what you need because otherwise, you will always feel that emptiness that you think only having someone can fill.

love is inscrutable
confusing
and complicated yet one of the only
feelings we search for

it's done
you're free
don't let the boredom
and loneliness to send you back

-   *you will heal*

a girl and her body is a relationship no man will ever
know but they act like they do
yet some act as if our skin is theirs to have a opinion
on as if they have to live within it
a relationship only the sisterhood would know of
they will never know the pain it causes
as this skin lives above our bones
as if we have been held under a microscope
layed upon a table
beautiful does not exist only if you can cross
everything of his checklist
because every roll turns into a hill
and every imperfection you say will eat us whole

-   *to be a woman*

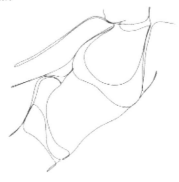

She Is Art

she sat there under the stars
alone and cold
trying to find the clarity
she had been searching a lifetime for
she sat there and prayed you were the one
how could it be anyone else
she prayed you were the man
she would walk down the alie with
but she also prayed
for a reason to leave
maybe that was all the clarity she ever needed

for him
she was just a chapter in his book
while he was the title of hers

we live in a generation where
when you're in love
you're free to touch each other
romantically
intimately
emotionally
but their phone
well it's private

narcissistic relationships

you won't realize until the very end that they have
been lying to you the entire time
right from the beginning
then it hits you
you were in love with a complete illusion
a total lie and a fraud
you were in love with their mask

"if they wanted to they would"

true, but also not
just because someone wants you
wants to text you
wants to hug you

doesn't mean they will
people force themselves to move on
that person will force themselves to leave you alone
they will force themselves to cut contact
but if they knew that you were special they would

you don't truly love someone
until they have hurt you
and you still think of them as the greatest person
in the whole world

- *love is the most violent act*

moving on isn't about not loving
or forgetting them
it is having that strength to say
i still love you
but you're not worth this pain

once you stop thinking sexually about people
you realize most of them aren't worth anything

-   *think who you are*
spending your time and energy on

i search for the moment
i wait for the day
i will see my own love in someone's eyes

-   *love me, how i love you*

i am afraid to love
thinking all love stories will turn out
much like yours
i am afraid of love
thinking everyone will love me
how you loved me

we live in a generation
where you can undress someone
with your eyes

-   *porn kills love*

sometimes their "apology"
comes too late when it is not
needed or wanted

- *your actions will always
  speak louder than your words*

i find peace in knowing
everything happens for a reason
if you weren't made for me
then i must've been meant for someone else

- *letting go*

she will be a heartbreaker

says says a drunk uncle at the family gathering,
as his niece just discovered make up for the first
time, "all the boys will love her"
replied the girl's aunt.

as she pulls down her pretty pink dress and wipes her
makeup off.
and a few years later, now getting whistled at the bus
station, the girl you said would be a heartbreaker
worries that if she doesn't wear makeup she won't be
an object of desire.

"a boy at school pulled my hair today" says the girl
with a frown of confusion, one of her pigtails was
looser than the other. "boys will be boys"
her teacher says. now she looks behind her when
walking alone, just in case boys will be boys

the girl you told those things to can not convince that
boy "no" is a full sentence, that's just how he was
brought up, they say
he hurt me, she says with a tear rolling down her
cheek. someone looks back at her and says, "oh
honey, what did you do?"

you cannot shame
yourself into change

and eventually
there was no set of chemicals that suddenly
put me on top of the world for days on end
there was not a person that made all my problems
fade away with their touch
there was nothing
just an empty void of nothingness

-   *i am simply just existing again*

if they left
if they hurt you
but it opened a sense of realization
a sense of clarity
that is a win you did not lose

-    *take it as a win*

"stop asking people for directions to places they have never been"

- *glennon doyle*

writing has healed the most vulnerable parts of me
the parts of me that i am yet to talk about

-    healing

you had all of me
every piece
every cell
until you didn't
but there is still a piece of me still belongs to you
i cannot let you know that
being unconditionally yours knowing
i'd always be there but i just can't hate you
i would love you forever if it were up to me

- *a love you will never touch*

it is going to hurt
every person you lowered yourself for
every person that took advantage of your kindness
the second you begin healing

sometimes you will have to give up
and let go of people not because you want to
but because you know you need to
because they only love you when it is a convenience
to them

-   *and i gave up on you*

i once looked at you and felt everything
and now i feel nothing

-    *ironically it makes me sad*

i think something is wrong with me
she says
i hide my love
i cover my ends
trust no one they said
so she didn't
you're cold
distant
numb they said
"you said trust no one"

i don't want you to see the emptiness that is held
within me
i don't want you to fill the empty parts of me
or make me feel whole
i want to be whole on my own

how do you turn a cold soul
so soft to be at peace with you

- *if you were at peace*

sometimes he will lie
sometimes he will pretend your the one falling apart
just so he doesn't feel bad
about what he is doing to you
just so he doesn't feel guilty
about how he is breaking you

-   *and he will*

simply you
don't worry about what they are saying about you
what they think about you
if they are going to make fun of how you did your
hair today or how you will do it tomorrow
you are your biggest commitment
focus on your awareness
your weirdness
focus on loving your insecurities
focus on becoming deeply connected to yourself

- *focus on becoming*
  the best person you can be for yourself

i will not beg to be in your life
i will not beg for you to build me in your life
i will not beg for your time

-   *i will not beg for you to love me*

you have to be strong for yourself
you have to look out for yourself
because if you don't
who will

love yourself
before you love anyone else

allow yourself to feel the hurt
the pain
the heartache
it is in our blood to feel
allow yourself to open up and be free

- growth

you need to fall
before you learn how to fly

- be patient

and in the end you realized that
none of them are special
it was just your image you made of them
that made them seem special

your art
your writing
is not about how many people like it
it's not about if people understand it

if it heals the most unhealed parts of you
the parts you don't talk about
if it heals your soul
your heart and all the in between
that is what matters

you are lovable
don't ever base your self worth
in the hands of someone who doesn't see the value
or beauty within you

you are heard, you are seen
you are everything you've ever needed.

ABOUT

She is art a collection of quotes and poetry
touching on
girlhood to womanhood
femininity
love
loss
and heartache
separated into four chapters, each touching on a
different kind of pain, each serving a different
purpose all through the lens of a woman perspective
She is art takes the reader through the journey of
some of the most hidden and intimate parts of
womanhood.
she is art,
you are art
womanhood is beautiful
and you are beautiful

She Is Art

Made in the USA
Monee, IL
01 January 2024

50900555R00125